Behavioral Finance and Investor Psychology

Alex Thompson

Published by Side Hustle Success, 2023.

BEHAVIORAL FINANCE AND INVESTOR PSYCHOLOGY

First edition. August 18, 2023.

ISBN: 979-8223096030

Written by Alex Thompson.

Also by Alex Thompson

Alex on Finance

Financial Freedom Roadmap - Achieving Early Retirement through the FIRE Movement

The Art of Strategic Innovation

Beyond Cash - The Evolution of Digital Payment Systems and the Future of Money

Preserving Wealth in Inflationary Times - Strategies for Protecting Your Financial Future

Standalone

Side Hustle Success: Unlocking Your Entrepreneurial Potential

Side Hustle Success: The Ultimate Guide to Passive and Financial Freedom

Mastering the Markets: Advanced Trading Strategies for Success and Ethical Trading Practices

Financial Fortitude

Mastering the Art of Upselling

The Financial Bullet Blueprint

Investing Demystified: A Beginner's Guide to Building Wealth in the Stock Market

Real Estate Riches: Building Wealth through Property Investment

How To Succeed as a Freelancer

Navigating Complex Waters: Advanced Strategies in Portfolio Management

Ethics in Quantitative Finance and Algorithmic Trading: Navigating Transparency, Fairness, and Accountability

Behavioral Finance and Investor Psychology

Table of Contents

Chapter 1: Introduction to Behavioral Finance and Investor Psychology

In the vast realm of finance, where numerical precision and analytical rigor reign supreme, an often understated yet immensely powerful force lurks beneath the surface – the intricate interplay between psychology and financial decision-making. At its core, this chapter introduces the captivating world of behavioral finance and investor psychology, a realm where human behavior and cognitive processes intertwine with economic choices to shape market dynamics, investment strategies, and the very foundation of financial systems.

Unveiling the Interplay: Where Psychology Meets Finance

In an idealized world, financial decisions would stem from rational assessment, unaffected by human emotions or biases. This notion forms the bedrock of traditional finance theory, where the rational agent model prevails. However, reality paints a more complex picture. Individuals often deviate from purely rational decision-making, influenced by an array of psychological factors that lend nuance and unpredictability to the financial landscape.

The Nature of Financial Decisions

To comprehend the depths of behavioral finance, one must first grasp the inherent challenges in modeling human behavior in financial contexts. Traditional economic theories assume individuals make choices based on complete information and rational analysis. Yet, real-world financial decisions are frequently made under conditions of uncertainty, incomplete information, and varying levels of rationality. This chapter dissects the tension between the theoretical assumptions of traditional finance and the behavioral realities that underpin decision-making.

Behavioral Finance: An Evolution

The emergence of behavioral finance marked a paradigm shift within the world of finance, elevating the importance of understanding human behavior in economic contexts. Traditionally, the efficient market hypothesis held sway, proposing that markets rapidly incorporate all available information, rendering it impossible to consistently outperform the market. However, anomalies and market behaviors inconsistent with this theory began to surface, prompting the exploration of alternative explanations rooted in behavioral psychology.

Investor Psychology: The Cognitive Landscape

At the heart of behavioral finance lies the captivating exploration of cognitive biases, those systematic deviations from rational judgment that lead individuals to make suboptimal decisions. These biases are cognitive shortcuts that help us navigate the overwhelming complexity of the world but can lead to distorted assessments of financial situations. Understanding these biases is critical to comprehending the deviations from rationality that characterize real-world financial decisions.

Cognitive Biases

Cognitive biases encompass a rich tapestry of mental shortcuts that often lead to irrational financial decisions. Anchoring and adjustment bias, for instance, causes individuals to rely heavily on initial pieces of information, anchoring their judgments to these starting points even when objectively irrelevant. Confirmation bias leads individuals to seek and prioritize information that confirms their pre-existing beliefs while disregarding contradictory evidence.

Emotions and Decision-Making

Emotions are an inherent part of the human experience, shaping not only personal interactions but also financial decisions. Fear, greed, and euphoria can drive individuals to make impulsive and suboptimal choices, often at odds with rational analysis. The fear of missing out (FOMO) can lead to hasty investment decisions, while the pain of losses amplifies risk aversion and can lead to irrational selling behavior.

The Power of Framing

How information is presented – or framed – significantly influences decision-making. Prospect theory, pioneered by Kahneman and Tversky, posits that individuals evaluate potential outcomes relative to a reference point, which can lead to different choices depending on the framing of the problem. This phenomenon showcases the malleability of decisions based on the context in which choices are presented.

The Journey Ahead

This chapter, a gateway to the fascinating world of behavioral finance and investor psychology, sets the stage for a transformative exploration. The subsequent chapters delve into cognitive biases, emotional influences, and their profound effects on market trends and investment choices. As we traverse this captivating landscape, we'll unravel the intricate threads binding human psychology to financial outcomes. Prepare to journey into the depths of the mind's impact on the markets, where rationality and emotion entwine to shape the financial landscape.

Evolution of Behavioral Finance and its Relevance in Today's Markets

The evolution of behavioral finance has been nothing short of revolutionary, reshaping our understanding of financial decision-making and unraveling the complexities that underlie seemingly rational economic choices. In the ever-evolving tapestry of financial markets, the relevance of behavioral finance stands as a testament to the intricate interplay between human psychology and the dynamics of modern economies.

Tracing the Path of Evolution

The journey of behavioral finance began as a reaction to the limitations of traditional finance theories, which largely assumed that individuals consistently make rational decisions based on complete information. However, empirical evidence unveiled discrepancies between theoretical predictions and real-world behavior, prompting scholars to explore the psychological underpinnings that drive financial choices.

The Birth of Behavioral Biases

One of the foundational pillars of behavioral finance is the recognition of cognitive biases – systematic deviations from rational decision-making that arise from mental shortcuts. As pioneering researchers like Daniel Kahneman and Amos Tversky unearthed these biases, a new dimension of understanding emerged. Biases such as overconfidence, loss aversion, and framing effects highlighted the complexity of human judgment and paved the way for a more comprehensive approach to financial analysis.

Market Anomalies and Aberrations

The embrace of behavioral finance was further fueled by the discovery of market anomalies that defied the predictions of traditional financial models. Phenomena like the momentum effect, where past winners tend to outperform past losers, contradicted efficient market hypotheses and indicated that psychological factors played a pivotal role in asset pricing and market dynamics.

Relevance in Today's Markets

The relevance of behavioral finance in today's markets cannot be overstated. As financial systems become more interconnected and technology enables rapid information dissemination, understanding the psychological forces at play has never been more crucial. Behavioral biases continue to influence investment decisions, contributing to market inefficiencies and providing opportunities for astute investors to exploit mispricings.

Behavioral Factors in Volatility

Volatility, often seen as a manifestation of market sentiment, is not solely driven by rational analysis. Emotional reactions to news, events, and macroeconomic trends can lead to rapid shifts in asset prices that are not easily explained by traditional models. By acknowledging the emotional undercurrents that fuel volatility, behavioral finance sheds light on market movements that might otherwise appear irrational.

Investor Behavior and Herd Mentality

The phenomenon of herd behavior, where individuals follow the actions of the majority, is a hallmark of investor psychology. The recent explosion of social media and online forums has amplified this behavior, leading to sudden and dramatic shifts in asset prices driven by the collective sentiments of the crowd. Understanding the dynamics of herd behavior is crucial for investors navigating the tumultuous waters of today's markets.

Algorithmic Trading and Behavioral Insights

Even in the realm of algorithmic trading, where machines execute trades at lightning speeds, behavioral insights are valuable. Algorithms may be programmed to exploit the predictable patterns of human behavior, driving short-term market movements. Recognizing these patterns and building algorithms that account for the biases of human traders can yield a significant advantage in high-frequency trading.

The Road Ahead

As markets continue to evolve in response to technological advancements and global dynamics, behavioral finance remains an indispensable tool for unraveling the intricacies of financial decision-making. From individual investors to institutional giants, the understanding of behavioral biases and psychological drivers has become a cornerstone of success in today's complex financial landscape. By acknowledging the role of human psychology in economic choices, we open doors to a more holistic comprehension of market trends, volatility, and the interconnected forces that shape our financial world.

Overview of Cognitive Biases, Emotions, and their Impact on Financial Decisions

The landscape of financial decision-making is not a sterile realm of cold calculations and logical deductions; it's a vibrant tapestry woven with the threads of human cognition and emotion. This chapter delves into the intricate web of cognitive biases and emotions, unraveling their profound impact on the choices individuals make within the realm of finance and investments.

Navigating the Cognitive Landscape

Cognitive biases, those subtle mental shortcuts that guide our judgments, are pervasive in every facet of life. Within the financial realm, they play an equally influential role, steering decisions away from purely rational paths. Understanding the various cognitive biases is akin to reading the invisible script that shapes financial choices.

Anchoring and Adjustment Bias

One of the most striking cognitive biases is the anchoring and adjustment bias, where initial pieces of information serve as reference points, anchoring subsequent decisions. In financial scenarios, this bias can lead investors to anchor on historical prices or initial valuations, often neglecting fundamental shifts that may warrant a different valuation.

Loss Aversion and Prospect Theory

The potent emotion of loss aversion is rooted in our evolutionary past, where avoiding losses held survival significance. Prospect theory, championed by Kahneman and Tversky, explains how individuals evaluate potential gains and losses relative to a reference point. The pain of a loss is often more pronounced than the pleasure of an equivalent gain, leading to suboptimal decisions.

Confirmation Bias and Overconfidence

Confirmation bias and overconfidence are close companions, nudging individuals to seek information that validates their pre-existing beliefs while dismissing conflicting evidence. Overconfidence, the illusion of greater knowledge and predictive ability, can drive investors to make overly risky decisions based on inflated self-assessment.

Emotions in Financial Decision-Making

Emotions color every aspect of life, and finance is no exception. The realm of investing often witnesses a symphony of emotions – from the euphoria of gains to the despair of losses. Emotions can distort judgment, amplify biases, and cloud rational assessment, leading to decisions that may not align with long-term goals.

Fear and Greed: The Twin Forces

Fear and greed are the twin engines that power much of investor behavior. The fear of losses can lead to impulsive selling during market downturns, while the greed for higher returns can drive investors into speculative and risky investments. Recognizing these emotional undercurrents is essential for making well-informed decisions.

Herding Behavior and Groupthink

The inclination to follow the crowd, known as herding behavior, is another manifestation of emotional influence. It can lead to market bubbles, where euphoria propels prices to unsustainable levels, and eventually, to market crashes when the collective sentiment shifts. Groupthink, the desire for conformity within a group, can stifle dissenting viewpoints and exacerbate irrational decisions.

Behavioral Finance and Investment Strategies

The impact of cognitive biases and emotions on financial decisions goes beyond theory; it shapes investment strategies and market trends. Momentum trading, for example, exploits the behavioral tendency for past winners to continue winning, while contrarian strategies capitalize on the overreaction of investors to recent news or events.

Navigating the Emotional Minefield

Recognizing these biases and emotions is the first step toward navigating the emotional minefield of investing. By peering beneath the surface and understanding the psychological currents that underlie financial choices, investors can make more informed and rational decisions, steering their portfolios toward greater success.

Chapter 2: Cognitive Biases and Decision-Making

Anchoring and Adjustment Bias: How Initial References Influence Decisions

The human mind is a remarkable instrument, capable of processing vast amounts of information and making decisions in a fraction of a second. However, this efficiency comes at a cost – the mind often resorts to cognitive shortcuts, or biases, that can lead to deviations from rational decision-making. Anchoring and adjustment bias is a fascinating cognitive phenomenon that showcases how our initial references can significantly impact the choices we make, especially within the realm of finance and investments.

The Anchoring Effect: Setting the Stage

Anchoring is a cognitive bias that occurs when individuals rely too heavily on the first piece of information they encounter when making decisions. This initial reference point, the "anchor," serves as a mental benchmark against which subsequent information is assessed. Whether it's a price tag, a historical valuation, or an analyst's estimate, the anchoring effect can distort judgments and lead to suboptimal choices.

Anchoring in Financial Decision-Making

In the financial arena, anchoring and adjustment bias can be a powerful force. Consider an investor evaluating a stock's potential value based on its current market price. If the stock recently experienced a sharp price increase, the investor may anchor on this elevated price and perceive it as the "correct" valuation, leading to decisions that might not align with the company's fundamentals.

The Pitfalls of Adjustment

While anchoring introduces the reference point, adjustment bias comes into play as individuals adjust their decisions from this anchor. However, the adjustment is often insufficient, leading to decisions that remain influenced by the original anchor. This phenomenon highlights the asymmetry between anchoring and adjustment, resulting in biased decisions that stray from rational assessments.

Mitigating Anchoring Bias

Recognizing and mitigating anchoring and adjustment bias is essential for making sound financial decisions. One approach is to deliberately seek out alternative reference points, decoupling decisions from the initial anchor. Additionally, employing systematic valuation methodologies and maintaining a disciplined investment process can help counteract the undue influence of anchoring.

Overcoming Anchoring in Investment

Anchoring bias can be particularly pronounced in investment scenarios where historical prices, past valuations, or expert forecasts act as anchors. To overcome this bias, investors can adopt a more comprehensive valuation approach that considers a range of fundamental factors rather than fixating on a single anchor. Diversifying information sources and consulting different experts can also help to create a more balanced perspective.

The Broader Implications

Beyond individual decisions, the anchoring and adjustment bias has broader implications for financial markets. Collective anchoring can lead to market bubbles, where prices become detached from fundamentals due to the persistence of an anchor. The subsequent adjustment phase can then result in sharp market corrections as the anchor is abandoned.

Cultivating Cognitive Agility

Cognitive biases like anchoring and adjustment are not weaknesses of the mind but rather inherent shortcuts that have evolved to help us navigate complex environments. However, in the world of finance, where rational analysis is paramount, recognizing and mitigating these biases is crucial. By cultivating cognitive agility and approaching decisions with awareness, investors can free themselves from the gravitational pull of initial references, enabling more rational and informed choices that stand up to the complexities of financial markets.

Confirmation Bias: The Tendency to Seek Information That Confirms Pre-existing Beliefs

The human mind is a remarkable pattern-seeking machine, designed to make sense of a vast and often overwhelming sea of information. However, this mental efficiency comes with a subtle pitfall – the confirmation bias. This chapter dives into the intricate workings of confirmation bias, shedding light on how our innate desire to validate pre-existing beliefs can influence financial decisions and shape investment outcomes.

The Quest for Validation

Confirmation bias, at its core, reflects our inclination to seek out information that supports our existing beliefs while dismissing or minimizing contrary evidence. It's like a mental filter that highlights data that aligns with what we already think, inadvertently creating a skewed view of reality.

In the Financial Arena

The financial arena is a breeding ground for confirmation bias. Investors often have specific beliefs about the market, specific stocks, or economic trends. When seeking information to validate these beliefs, they unconsciously filter out information that challenges their views. This can lead to a distorted perception of market conditions and hinder the ability to make objective investment decisions.

Investor Behavior Amplified

Confirmation bias doesn't merely shape individual decisions; it also affects collective market behavior. When a critical mass of investors share a common belief and selectively focus on information that confirms it, market trends can become self-fulfilling prophecies. This amplification of investor behavior based on biased beliefs can lead to exaggerated market swings and bubbles.

Enhancing the Illusion

In the age of information overload, confirmation bias thrives. Online forums, social media, and news outlets provide endless content tailored to individual preferences, further entrenching existing beliefs. Investors unwittingly surround themselves with echo chambers of like-minded opinions, unknowingly reinforcing their confirmation bias.

Mitigating Confirmation Bias

Recognizing and mitigating confirmation bias is crucial for making sound financial decisions. Active steps can be taken to counteract this bias:

1. Seek Contrary Opinions: Actively seek out viewpoints that challenge your existing beliefs. Engaging with diverse perspectives can help broaden your understanding of market dynamics.

2. Maintain a Devil's Advocate Approach: When analyzing an investment opportunity, intentionally look for reasons why it might fail rather than just reasons why it might succeed.

3. Document Assumptions: Write down your assumptions and beliefs before conducting research. This can create a record of your initial stance, allowing you to objectively assess whether new information truly challenges your beliefs.

4. Engage in Continuous Learning: Embrace a mindset of constant learning and adaptability. By acknowledging that your knowledge is never complete, you're more likely to be receptive to new information.

5. Stay Humble: Recognize that even seasoned investors can fall prey to confirmation bias. Maintaining humility about the limits of your own knowledge can open doors to more balanced decision-making.

Breaking the Bias

Confirmation bias is a formidable force that can distort financial decisions and market behavior. By understanding its mechanisms and actively working to counteract it, investors can strive for a more balanced and objective approach to decision-making. In a world awash with information, the ability to discern the truth from the noise becomes paramount, enabling investors to navigate the complexities of the financial landscape with greater clarity and accuracy.

Overconfidence Bias: The Illusion of Superior Knowledge and Prediction Abilities

Introduction

Overconfidence bias is a cognitive bias that leads individuals to overestimate their own abilities, knowledge, and predictive accuracy. It creates a psychological illusion that one possesses a superior grasp of information and decision-making capabilities, which can significantly impact financial decisions and investment outcomes.

The Illusion of Expertise

At the heart of overconfidence bias is the tendency to believe that one's judgments are more accurate and insightful than they truly are. This can manifest in various ways:

1. **Overestimation of Skill:** Investors may believe they possess superior skills in stock picking, market timing, or financial analysis, leading them to take riskier positions or engage in excessive trading.

2. **Overoptimism:** Investors may exhibit unwarranted optimism about their investment outcomes, underestimating potential risks and focusing solely on potential gains.

3. **Overprecision:** Overconfidence bias often extends to the precision of predictions. Investors might express high confidence in specific price targets, economic indicators, or market trends, despite the inherent uncertainty of financial markets.

Biased Decision-Making

Overconfidence bias can distort decision-making processes and lead to suboptimal outcomes:

1. Increased Trading Activity: Overconfident investors might engage in frequent trading, assuming they can outperform the market. However, higher trading costs and potential losses can erode returns.

2. Ignoring Contrary Evidence: Investors under the sway of overconfidence bias may dismiss information that challenges their beliefs, leading to a narrow view of market dynamics.

3. Neglecting Risk Management: Overconfidence can lead to underestimating risks or disregarding the importance of diversification and risk management strategies.

Market Implications

The collective impact of overconfidence bias can affect market trends and behavior:

1. Bubbles and Exuberance: A critical mass of overconfident investors can contribute to market bubbles, where prices become detached from fundamentals due to excessive optimism.

2. Volatility: Overconfident trading can lead to increased market volatility as participants react to their overly optimistic or pessimistic predictions.

3. Amplified Trends: Overconfidence can amplify trends and market momentum, as investors interpret their predictions as undeniable signals of market direction.

Mitigating Overconfidence Bias

Recognizing and mitigating overconfidence bias is vital for making rational financial decisions:

1. Maintain Humility: Acknowledge the inherent uncertainty in financial markets and the limitations of individual expertise.

2. Seek Diverse Perspectives: Engage with professionals, experts, and investors who hold different viewpoints, helping to challenge your own assumptions.

3. Embrace Learning: Approach every decision as an opportunity to learn. Keep track of your predictions and revisit them to assess their accuracy.

4. Evaluate Past Decisions: Reflect on past decisions to identify instances where overconfidence bias might have influenced your choices.

5. Employ Risk Management: Implement risk management strategies, diversification, and portfolio construction techniques that account for potential errors in judgment.

Conclusion

Overconfidence bias is a powerful force that can distort financial decision-making and shape market behavior. Awareness of this bias and an ongoing commitment to self-awareness and continuous learning can help investors navigate the complexities of the financial landscape with greater prudence and rationality. By balancing confidence with humility, investors can make more informed and rational decisions that align with their long-term financial goals.

Availability Bias: The Influence of Easily Recalled Information on Decision-Making

In the intricate tapestry of financial decision-making, cognitive biases exert a profound influence on our choices. One particularly potent bias is the availability bias, which sheds light on how the ease of recalling information can subtly sway our financial decisions and contribute to market trends.

The availability bias is a cognitive shortcut that our brains employ, known as the availability heuristic. This heuristic hinges on the notion that if information is easily recalled, it must hold greater significance or validity. This mental mechanism, while often helpful for quick decisions, can lead to systematic errors when applied to the complex landscape of finance.

In the realm of finance, availability bias plays a pivotal role in shaping our perceptions of risk and reward. It can significantly impact the choices investors make, often in subtle yet pervasive ways. One striking manifestation is the amplification of recent events. Information from recent news and events is vivid and tends to be more readily accessible in our memory. As a result, investors might give undue weight to these recent market developments when making decisions. The allure of immediacy, however, can distort the comprehensive view that informed decision-making requires.

Another captivating facet of availability bias lies in the emotional magnitude of events. Dramatic and emotionally charged events are not only more memorable but also tend to exert a more significant influence on our decision-making process. This psychological phenomenon can lead to skewed assessments of risk and potential outcomes. The information that tugs at our emotions can overshadow more subtle, but perhaps more relevant, considerations.

The tendency to neglect historical context is another facet of availability bias. Investors under its sway might disregard historical data and trends in favor of the most recent, vivid information. This inclination can be particularly pronounced during periods of market turbulence when the sensationalism of the present moment eclipses the wisdom of the past. The consequence is a distorted sense of market dynamics that can impede optimal decision-making.

The impact of availability bias doesn't merely extend to individual decisions—it can shape market behavior on a larger scale. News outlets often prioritize and highlight negative events, contributing to an overemphasis on pessimistic perspectives even when market conditions are more nuanced. Availability bias can also reinforce existing market trends as investors gravitate toward recent successes or failures when crafting their investment strategies. Additionally, the bias can strengthen the hold of consensus views when they align with readily available information, creating a self-perpetuating cycle of bias and belief.

Mitigating the impact of availability bias requires a deliberate and conscious effort. Actively seeking diverse information sources is paramount in order to ensure a well-rounded perspective that transcends the sway of recent events. Integrating historical data and long-term trends into your decision-making process can provide a more balanced view of market dynamics. Consciously questioning the basis of recalled information whenever making a decision is a practice that can counteract the influence of availability bias. Prioritizing data-driven analysis and research that rely on a comprehensive set of facts, rather than relying solely on easily recalled information, is essential.

Availability bias is a silent force that shapes financial decisions and can inadvertently lead us astray. By understanding its mechanisms and taking proactive steps to counter its effects, investors can navigate the complex landscape of finance with greater clarity and sound judgment. Striving for a holistic understanding, one that transcends the allure of easily recalled information, is a cornerstone of making informed and rational financial decisions.

Chapter 3: Emotions in Investment

Fear of Missing Out (FOMO): The Emotional Drive Behind Herd Behavior

In the intricate world of investment, emotions are as much a part of the equation as numbers and data. Among the myriad of emotions that influence financial decisions, the Fear of Missing Out (FOMO) stands out as a potent force that drives herd behavior and shapes market trends. This chapter delves deep into the psychology of FOMO, exploring its roots, manifestations, and the profound impact it has on investment choices.

The FOMO Phenomenon: A Psychological Tug

Fear of Missing Out is a sentiment that transcends the realm of finance. It's a psychological response to the apprehension that others are benefiting from opportunities that we might be passing up. In the context of investment, FOMO manifests as an overwhelming desire to join the crowd, to participate in a trend or asset that appears to be soaring.

The Herd Behavior Connection

FOMO is a driving force behind herd behavior, the phenomenon where individuals mimic the actions of a larger group, often without fully understanding the rationale behind those actions. When FOMO takes hold, investors rush to invest in assets that are seemingly on the rise, fearing that they will miss out on significant gains.

Emotional Triggers: The Fuel for FOMO

FOMO is fueled by a complex interplay of emotions:

1. Envy and Regret: Envy for those who seem to be capitalizing on an opportunity can create a sense of regret for not having acted sooner. This emotional cocktail can lead to impulsive decisions driven by the need to catch up.

2. Social Validation: The need for social validation and acceptance plays a role in FOMO. Investing in what everyone else seems to be investing in provides a sense of belonging and reassurance.

3. Information Overload: The constant stream of information and news in today's digital age intensifies FOMO. Investors fear that missing out on a hot tip or trend could result in missed profits.

4. Anchoring Bias: FOMO can be triggered by an anchoring bias, where investors fixate on a reference point, such as a recent price high, and fear missing the opportunity to buy before prices rise further.

Market Implications

FOMO doesn't just impact individual investors—it can collectively shape market dynamics:

1. Amplification of Trends: FOMO can amplify market trends, creating bubbles and volatility as investors pile into certain assets. This can lead to price distortions and increased market risks.

2. Behavior-Driven Cycles: FOMO-driven cycles can perpetuate themselves. Investors buy into rising assets due to FOMO, which drives prices higher. Subsequently, as prices peak or decline, fear turns into panic selling, creating a self-fulfilling prophecy.

3. Fragility and Systemic Risks: Overreliance on FOMO-driven investment decisions can result in fragile markets susceptible to rapid shifts in sentiment and destabilizing sell-offs.

Navigating the FOMO Trap

Mitigating the impact of FOMO requires a disciplined and informed approach:

1. Focus on Fundamentals: Ground your investment decisions in solid fundamentals rather than succumbing to FOMO-driven impulses.

2. Long-Term Perspective: Maintain a long-term perspective and avoid making rash decisions based on short-term trends.

3. Education and Research: Invest time in understanding the assets you're considering, evaluating their potential and risks, and making informed decisions.

4. Diversification: Diversify your portfolio to reduce the impact of FOMO-driven decisions on your overall financial well-being.

5. Mindful Decision-Making: Be aware of your emotional triggers and practice mindful decision-making to counteract the influence of FOMO.

The Temptation and the Triumph

Fear of Missing Out is a powerful emotional force that can lure even the most seasoned investors into making impulsive decisions. However, awareness and vigilance can enable investors to rise above the pull of FOMO. By understanding its psychological underpinnings, recognizing its impact on market trends, and developing strategies to counter its influence, investors can make more informed and rational choices. In a landscape where emotions can sway even the strongest strategies, navigating the FOMO trap is a testament to an investor's resilience and commitment to prudent decision-making.

Regret Aversion: How Avoiding Regret Influences Investment Choices

In the realm of investment, where uncertainty looms and outcomes are never guaranteed, the fear of experiencing regret exerts a powerful sway over decision-making. Regret aversion, a cognitive bias deeply rooted in our psychology, can significantly influence how we perceive risks, evaluate opportunities, and ultimately shape our investment choices.

The Psychology of Regret Aversion

Regret aversion is a natural response driven by our desire to minimize the pain of making choices that we might come to regret later. This bias is fueled by the fear of making a decision that will lead to unfavorable outcomes, often causing us to avoid actions that might result in future remorse. While seemingly protective, regret aversion can sometimes hinder rational decision-making, leading us to stay in our comfort zones and overlook potentially lucrative opportunities.

Avoiding the Pain of "I Should Have..."

Regret aversion has a profound impact on investment choices:

1. Inaction Bias: The bias frequently leads to a tendency of inaction—opting for the status quo or avoiding decisions altogether. This avoidance is driven by the hope of avoiding the emotional turmoil that accompanies realizing we missed out on a potentially profitable venture.

2. Anchoring and Missed Opportunities: Regret aversion can anchor us to past decisions, making us reluctant to revise our strategies even when new information suggests better alternatives. This can lead to missed investment opportunities that could yield more favorable outcomes.

3. The Paradox of Decision Timing: Investors influenced by regret aversion might procrastinate decisions, often to their detriment. The longer we delay, the more the regret associated with not acting earlier compounds, leading to a vicious cycle of indecision.

4. Short-Term Focus: Regret aversion can narrow our focus, causing us to concentrate on avoiding short-term losses rather than considering longer-term growth and potential gains.

5. Herding Behavior: The fear of regret can trigger herding behavior, causing us to follow the crowd and avoid standing out even when our analysis suggests otherwise.

Taming Regret Aversion

Mitigating the impact of regret aversion requires a multi-pronged approach:

1. Rational Analysis: Overcoming regret aversion starts with rational analysis. Evaluate opportunities objectively based on data, trends, and informed research, rather than being driven solely by the fear of regret.

2. Embrace Learning: Embrace a mindset of continuous learning. Understand that setbacks and occasional missteps are part of the investment journey and can provide valuable lessons for future decisions.

3. Diversification: Diversifying your investment portfolio can help alleviate the intensity of regret associated with any single investment decision. A diverse portfolio mitigates the impact of any one poor choice.

4. Long-Term Vision: Adopting a long-term perspective can help counteract the short-term focus induced by regret aversion. Realize that markets experience fluctuations, but over time, quality investments tend to yield positive returns.

5. Recognize Opportunity Costs: Understand that avoiding a decision due to fear of regret carries its own set of opportunity costs. Inaction itself can lead to missed opportunities that could have provided growth.

6. Embrace Regret as Part of the Process: Embrace the fact that some level of regret is inherent in investing. Accept it as a natural element of decision-making, and recognize that not every choice will lead to optimal outcomes.

Balancing Caution and Growth

Regret aversion is a double-edged sword—an emotion that protects us from the pain of potential regret while simultaneously impeding us from fully embracing opportunities for growth. By recognizing the influence of this bias, understanding its mechanisms, and developing strategies to counter its impact, investors can strike a balance between prudent caution and the pursuit of fruitful investment endeavors. In a realm where avoiding regret often means embracing opportunity, the art of taming regret aversion becomes a critical skill in the investor's toolkit.

Prospect Theory: Understanding Risk Perception and Framing in Investment Decisions

The human mind's perception of risk and its subsequent influence on decision-making is a complex interplay of cognitive and emotional factors. Prospect theory, a cornerstone of behavioral economics, sheds light on how individuals evaluate and make choices in situations involving uncertainty, especially in the realm of investment. This chapter delves into the intricacies of prospect theory, exploring its components, implications, and the profound impact it has on framing investment decisions.

The Basis of Prospect Theory

Developed by psychologists Daniel Kahneman and Amos Tversky in the 1970s, prospect theory challenged the conventional economic assumption that individuals make decisions solely based on rational assessments of expected outcomes. Prospect theory posits that people's decisions are influenced not only by the potential outcomes but also by how those outcomes are framed and presented.

Risk Aversion and the Value Function

At the core of prospect theory is the S-shaped value function, which illustrates how individuals perceive gains and losses in relation to a reference point. The value function demonstrates that individuals are typically risk-averse when faced with potential gains, often valuing the certainty of a smaller gain over the uncertain chance of a larger gain. Conversely, when confronted with potential losses, individuals tend to embrace risk, opting for uncertainty to avoid certain losses.

Framing Effects and Investment Choices

Prospect theory introduces two critical framing effects that shape investment decisions:

1. **Loss Aversion:** Loss aversion describes the phenomenon where individuals feel the pain of losses more acutely than the pleasure of equivalent gains. This tendency can lead to risk aversion in situations where losses are anticipated, even if the potential gains are more substantial.

2. **Reference Dependence:** Prospect theory highlights how our perception of outcomes is relative to a reference point. This point can vary depending on how the situation is framed. For instance, when an investment is presented as a sure gain, individuals are more likely to take a risk-averse stance. On the other hand, when the same investment is framed as avoiding a potential loss, individuals are more inclined to take risks.

Implications for Investment Decisions

Prospect theory has profound implications for investment choices:

1. Framing and Decision Bias: The way investment opportunities are framed can significantly influence our choices. Investors may be risk-averse when facing potential gains (choosing certain, smaller gains) but risk-seeking when confronting potential losses (opting for uncertain, potentially smaller losses).

2. Loss Aversion and Selling Behavior: Loss aversion can lead to suboptimal selling behavior. Investors might hold onto losing investments for too long, hoping to recover losses rather than cutting their losses.

3. Diversification and Risk Management: Investors' perception of risk and gain can lead to suboptimal portfolio construction. Understanding the framing effects of prospect theory can guide investors toward building well-diversified portfolios that align with their goals.

4. Behavioral Biases and Market Trends: Prospect theory, along with other behavioral biases, can contribute to the formation of market trends. As individuals react to framed information, these collective decisions can shape market movements.

Navigating Prospect Theory's Influence

Navigating the influence of prospect theory requires a comprehensive approach:

1. Awareness: Recognize the impact of framing effects and reference points on your decision-making. Question how information is presented and consider how your choices might differ with alternative frames.

2. Long-Term Perspective: Adopting a long-term perspective can help mitigate the short-term emotional influences of prospect theory. Understand that investment decisions should be grounded in thorough analysis and a comprehensive strategy.

3. Risk Management: Integrate the lessons of prospect theory into your risk management strategies. Understand how framing can influence risk perception and adjust your risk management strategies accordingly.

4. Education and Analysis: Equip yourself with a solid understanding of prospect theory and other behavioral biases. Engage in thorough research and analysis before making investment decisions.

Harnessing Insights for Better Choices

Prospect theory provides valuable insights into the complexities of human decision-making in the context of investments. By understanding the framing effects, loss aversion, and reference dependence that underlie prospect theory, investors can make more informed, rational, and balanced decisions. While our minds are inherently susceptible to these cognitive biases, the awareness and application of prospect theory's principles can empower investors to navigate the dynamic landscape of finance with greater clarity and foresight.

Loss Aversion: The Psychological Impact of Losses on Decision-Making

In the intricate tapestry of human decision-making, the fear of loss often wields a more potent influence than the allure of gain. Loss aversion, a foundational concept in behavioral finance, delves into the powerful psychological inclination to avoid losses at the cost of potential gains. This chapter unveils the complexities of loss aversion, exploring its psychological underpinnings, manifestations in financial choices, and its overarching impact on investment decision-making.

The Emotional Weight of Loss

At the heart of loss aversion lies a fundamental psychological phenomenon: the emotional weight of losses is far greater than the satisfaction of equivalent gains. This phenomenon was first theorized and empirically demonstrated by Nobel laureates Daniel Kahneman and Amos Tversky in their groundbreaking work on prospect theory.

The Prospect Theory Framework

Prospect theory describes how individuals make choices between alternatives that involve risk and uncertainty. Loss aversion is a key component of prospect theory, emphasizing that people experience the pain of loss more acutely than the pleasure of gain. This asymmetry gives rise to the following tendencies:

1. Seeking Certainty: Loss aversion often leads individuals to opt for certain but smaller gains rather than taking a risk on uncertain but potentially larger gains. This desire for certainty can overshadow rational assessments of probability.

2. Holding On to Losing Investments: Loss aversion can lead investors to hold on to losing investments for longer than they should, in the hope of recouping losses. This behavior can result in suboptimal portfolio performance.

3. Selling Winners Prematurely: On the flip side, individuals might sell investments that have gained in value too soon to lock in the perceived gain and avoid potential future losses.

4. Reference Points and Decision-Making: Loss aversion is often tied to the concept of reference points—individuals compare their current status to a reference point and assess whether they are better off or worse off. Losses are measured against this reference point, intensifying the aversion to losses.

Overcoming the Bias

Recognizing and addressing loss aversion is pivotal for effective investment decision-making:

1. Rational Analysis: When evaluating investment opportunities, focus on objective data and analysis rather than allowing emotional biases to drive decisions.

2. Long-Term Perspective: Adopt a long-term perspective that emphasizes the overall performance of your portfolio rather than fixating on short-term losses.

3. Diversification: A well-diversified portfolio can help mitigate the impact of individual losses by spreading risk across various assets.

4. **Risk Management:** Incorporate risk management strategies that account for the psychological impact of losses. Setting stop-loss orders or predetermined exit points can help prevent losses from spiraling.

5. **Emotional Awareness:** Develop self-awareness of your emotional responses to losses. By acknowledging and managing these emotions, you can make more rational decisions.

6. **Focus on Goals:** Keep your investment goals at the forefront. Align your decisions with your long-term objectives rather than succumbing to short-term emotional impulses.

7. **Investment Education:** Educate yourself about behavioral biases like loss aversion. Knowledge can help you identify these biases when they arise and take steps to counteract them.

Embracing Loss as Part of Growth

Loss aversion is deeply rooted in our psychological makeup, often leading us to shy away from risks and remain in our comfort zones. However, it's important to recognize that losses are an inherent part of the investment journey. They can provide valuable learning experiences that contribute to a more informed and resilient investor. By understanding loss aversion and its impact, investors can strive for a balanced approach that acknowledges the emotional aspect of decision-making while prioritizing rational analysis, strategic planning, and a long-term perspective.

Chapter 4: Bubbles, Panics, and Market Trends

Tulip Mania and Other Historical Market Bubbles: Insights into Irrational Exuberance

Market bubbles, those fascinating yet cautionary tales of exuberant speculation followed by sudden crashes, have been a recurring phenomenon throughout history. From the tulip mania of the 17th century to the dot-com bubble of the late 20th century, these episodes highlight the power of irrational exuberance and collective psychology in shaping market trends. This chapter journeys through some of history's most iconic bubbles, offering insights into the behavioral factors that fuel their rise, the emotions that sustain them, and the lessons they leave behind.

The Tulip Mania of the 17th Century: A Blooming Bubble

One of the earliest recorded market bubbles, tulip mania, swept through the Dutch Republic in the 1630s. Tulip bulbs, originally imported from the Ottoman Empire, became the objects of intense speculation. The prices of these bulbs skyrocketed to absurd levels, driven by factors such as scarcity, novelty, and societal status. The speculative frenzy eventually collapsed, leaving many investors with worthless bulbs.

The South Sea Bubble: A Tale of Speculation and Delusion

In the early 18th century, the South Sea Company captured the imagination of British investors with promises of lucrative returns from trade with South America. As share prices soared, driven by greed and the fear of missing out, investors were blinded to the company's lack of substantial assets. The bubble burst in 1720, causing financial ruin for many and leading to tighter regulations in the financial markets.

The Roaring Twenties and the Great Depression: A Tale of Excess and Collapse

The stock market boom of the 1920s in the United States saw investors riding a wave of optimism and speculation. The irrational exuberance of the era, characterized by easy credit and overvalued stocks, culminated in the 1929 crash that marked the onset of the Great Depression. The boom and bust cycle highlighted how emotional factors can lead to unsustainable market trends.

The Dot-Com Bubble: Technological Optimism and Its Fallout

The late 1990s witnessed the meteoric rise of internet-related stocks during the dot-com bubble. Investors were captivated by the allure of the digital revolution and the potential for astronomical gains. However, many of these companies lacked solid business models or profits. The bubble burst in 2000, leaving shattered portfolios and valuable lessons about the importance of fundamental analysis.

Behavioral Factors at Play

These historical bubbles illuminate several key behavioral factors that contribute to their formation:

1. **Herd Behavior:** The urge to follow the crowd and not miss out on perceived gains plays a pivotal role in the formation of bubbles. As more people invest, prices rise, reinforcing the perception of value.

2. **Fear of Missing Out (FOMO):** Investors driven by FOMO often succumb to the allure of quick riches, ignoring rational analysis and due diligence.

3. **Over-Optimism:** Irrational exuberance, characterized by unrealistic expectations and overestimation of potential gains, can distort perceptions of risk and reward.

4. **Groupthink:** The tendency to conform to prevailing opinions within a group can lead to a collective dismissal of dissenting views and a distorted assessment of risks.

Lessons from Bubbles

The study of historical bubbles offers valuable insights for investors:

1. Awareness: Recognize the signs of a speculative bubble, including rapid price escalation, excessive media coverage, and the emergence of new investment products.

2. Rational Analysis: Base investment decisions on thorough analysis of fundamentals rather than succumbing to hype and emotion.

3. Diversification: A well-diversified portfolio can help mitigate the impact of a bubble burst in any single asset or sector.

4. Long-Term Perspective: Adopt a long-term investment horizon that focuses on sustainable growth and fundamental value.

5. Balancing Emotion and Analysis: While emotions are a natural part of investing, ensure they are balanced with rational analysis and strategic planning.

6. Learning from History: Understanding the behavioral factors that contribute to bubbles can help investors navigate the market with greater awareness and prudence.

Navigating the Waves of Market Psychology

The stories of tulip mania, the South Sea Bubble, the Great Depression, and the dot-com bubble remind us that market trends are often shaped as much by collective psychology as by economic fundamentals. These historical bubbles underscore the potent interplay of fear, greed, and human nature in financial decision-making. By drawing lessons from the past, investors can develop a nuanced understanding of market psychology, strengthen their decision-making processes, and embark on a journey of informed and sustainable investing.

Behavioral Explanations for Market Panics and Crashes

Market panics and crashes are seismic events that disrupt financial stability, shatter investor confidence, and challenge the fundamental principles of rational decision-making. Traditional economic theories often struggle to explain the extreme volatility and irrational behavior witnessed during such episodes. However, behavioral finance offers a lens through which to understand the psychological underpinnings of these events. This chapter delves into the behavioral explanations for market panics and crashes, exploring how cognitive biases, herd behavior, and emotional contagion can ignite and intensify market turmoil.

The Herding Instinct and Contagion

One of the most prevalent explanations for market panics and crashes lies in the concept of herd behavior. Human beings possess a natural inclination to follow the actions of the crowd, especially in times of uncertainty. This herd behavior can lead to a domino effect where one investor's decision triggers a chain reaction of similar decisions.

1. Cascading Fear: During market panics, fear spreads like wildfire. When investors observe others selling rapidly, they interpret it as a signal of impending danger, prompting them to sell as well. This collective response can amplify the panic and lead to a rapid downward spiral in prices.

2. Information Cascades: Investors tend to rely on the actions of others as a shortcut for decision-making, rather than independently assessing the underlying fundamentals. As more people join the selling frenzy, others feel compelled to follow suit, creating an information cascade that drives prices further down.

3. Contagion: The emotional contagion that occurs during market panics leads to the spread of negative emotions such as fear, anxiety, and panic. Even investors who were not initially affected may succumb to the prevailing sentiment, leading to a market-wide stampede.

Cognitive Biases in Times of Crisis

Cognitive biases, deeply ingrained patterns of thought that can deviate from rationality, become exacerbated during periods of market turmoil. Several key biases play a role in driving market panics:

1. Loss Aversion: As discussed earlier, loss aversion intensifies the psychological impact of losses. When losses mount during a market crash, investors' decisions are driven more by fear of losing than by rational assessment.

2. Anchoring and Adjustment Bias: Investors may anchor their decisions to previous price levels, making it challenging for them to adjust their perceptions in the face of rapid declines.

3. Availability Bias: The vividness of recent market events can distort decision-making. Investors tend to overestimate the likelihood of events they have witnessed recently, leading to panic when those events are negative.

Emotion and Irrational Decision-Making

Emotion plays a central role in market panics and crashes, often driving investors to abandon rational analysis in favor of impulsive reactions:

1. Fear and Panic: Fear of loss, heightened by uncertainty, prompts investors to make hasty decisions. Panic can lead to indiscriminate selling, regardless of the underlying value of assets.

2. Over-Optimism and Denial: Paradoxically, periods of market euphoria can also lead to crashes. Investors become over-optimistic, downplaying risks and dismissing signs of an impending downturn until it's too late.

3. Cognitive Dissonance: When faced with conflicting information that challenges their beliefs, investors may experience cognitive dissonance, causing them to seek out information that aligns with their existing views rather than objectively evaluating the situation.

Learning and Adapting

Understanding the behavioral explanations for market panics and crashes can equip investors with tools to navigate such turbulent waters more effectively:

1. Emotional Discipline: Developing emotional resilience and discipline in times of crisis can prevent rash decisions driven by fear or panic.

2. Independent Analysis: Rely on rational analysis rather than herd behavior. Evaluate investment decisions based on fundamental factors rather than succumbing to the pull of the crowd.

3. Crisis Preparedness: Having a well-defined investment strategy that accounts for different market scenarios can provide a roadmap during turbulent times.

4. Contrarian Approach: While contrarian strategies carry their own risks, they can be effective in counteracting herd behavior. Buying when others are selling and vice versa requires a strong conviction in one's analysis.

5. Continuous Learning: Stay informed about behavioral biases and how they can influence decision-making. By recognizing these biases, you can mitigate their impact on your choices.

6. Long-Term Perspective: Maintaining a long-term perspective can help dampen the impact of short-term market panics. Focus on your investment goals and objectives rather than reacting to short-term fluctuations.

Navigating the Storms of Investor Behavior

Market panics and crashes are reminders that the financial markets are not just cold, rational machines driven by numbers and data. Human psychology and behavior play a crucial role in shaping the direction and magnitude of market movements. By delving into the behavioral explanations for market panics and crashes, investors can develop a deeper understanding of the forces at play, cultivate emotional discipline, and make more informed decisions that align with their long-term financial goals.

Momentum and Trend-Following Strategies: The Psychology Behind Riding Market Trends

In the world of finance, where uncertainty and complexity abound, the concept of momentum stands as a paradox. At its core, momentum investing involves capitalizing on the persistence of recent market trends, riding the wave of success as it carries assets higher. However, beneath this seemingly straightforward strategy lies a complex interplay of psychology, behavioral biases, and market dynamics that contribute to its effectiveness and challenges. This chapter dives deep into the psychology behind momentum and trend-following strategies, exploring why they work, the cognitive biases that fuel them, and the potential pitfalls that can arise from riding market trends.

The Allure of Momentum

Momentum, often referred to as the "trend is your friend," is a strategy that relies on the continuation of existing market trends. It defies the conventional wisdom of "buy low, sell high," instead suggesting that assets that have recently performed well are likely to continue performing well in the short term. This counterintuitive approach is rooted in several psychological and behavioral factors:

1. Herding Behavior: The bandwagon effect drives investors to follow the crowd. As an asset gains momentum, more investors jump on the trend, further fueling its rise.

2. Availability Bias: Investors tend to remember recent events more vividly, leading them to overweight the importance of recent price movements in their decisions.

3. Overconfidence: The success of recent trades can boost investors' confidence, making them more likely to believe that their predictions will continue to be accurate.

4. Anchoring and Adjustment: Anchoring to recent price levels can distort investors' perceptions, causing them to underestimate the potential for price changes in the opposite direction.

The Challenges of Momentum

While momentum strategies can be profitable, they are not without risks and challenges. The psychological drivers that underpin momentum can lead to bubbles and crashes, as well as amplification of market trends beyond their fundamentals:

1. Overvaluation and Bubbles: As investors chase momentum, prices can become detached from underlying fundamentals, resulting in overvaluation and the potential for market bubbles.

2. Reversal and Crashes: Momentum can persist until it doesn't. Sudden shifts in sentiment can trigger abrupt reversals, catching momentum investors off guard.

3. Herding and Feedback Loops: Excessive momentum can lead to herding behavior, which in turn can create feedback loops that amplify market movements in both directions.

4. Short-Term Focus: Momentum strategies are inherently short-term focused, which can lead to a disconnect between market trends and the long-term value of assets.

The Role of Behavioral Biases

Cognitive biases play a crucial role in the effectiveness of momentum strategies. Behavioral biases can lead to herding behavior and price momentum, creating opportunities for investors who are aware of these biases:

1. Confirmation Bias: Investors tend to seek information that confirms their existing beliefs about a trend's continuation, reinforcing their commitment to the strategy.

2. Anchoring: Investors anchor their expectations to recent prices, leading them to adjust their predictions incrementally rather than comprehensively reevaluating the trend.

3. Loss Aversion: Momentum strategies, built on the expectation of continued gains, can expose investors to the psychological pain of missed opportunities.

Navigating Momentum Strategies

Investors who choose to explore momentum and trend-following strategies should be mindful of the psychological factors at play:

1. Risk Management: Momentum strategies can be highly volatile. Implement robust risk management to mitigate the impact of reversals.

2. Diversification: A diversified portfolio can help offset the risks associated with focusing solely on momentum.

3. Timing: Timing is crucial in momentum strategies. Be prepared for the possibility of sudden reversals and consider employing technical indicators for entry and exit points.

4. Awareness of Biases: Recognize the cognitive biases that drive momentum strategies and remain vigilant against their influence on your decisions.

5. Long-Term vs. Short-Term: Consider whether a momentum strategy aligns with your investment horizon and goals. Short-term strategies may not suit all investors.

6. Fundamental Analysis: Combine momentum strategies with fundamental analysis to ensure that the underlying fundamentals of the assets align with their price movements.

7. Market Environment: Be aware of the broader market environment. Momentum strategies may perform differently in bull and bear markets.

Riding the Momentum Wave

Momentum and trend-following strategies tap into the intriguing psychology of market participants. Understanding the psychological factors that drive momentum can empower investors to make informed decisions, capitalize on trends, and navigate the complexities of market momentum. Whether one chooses to ride the wave of market trends or employs a more conservative approach, the insights gained from exploring momentum's psychological foundations can enhance decision-making and contribute to a more well-rounded investment strategy.

Chapter 5: Psychological Factors in Investment Styles

Value Investing: How Cognitive Biases Play a Role in Contrarian Strategies

Value investing, often described as "buying a dollar for 50 cents," is a time-tested investment approach that seeks to uncover hidden gems in the market by identifying undervalued assets. While value investing appears rational on the surface, it is intricately intertwined with the complexities of human psychology and behavioral biases. This chapter delves into the world of value investing, exploring the cognitive biases that both propel and challenge this investment style, and how understanding these psychological factors can enhance the application of contrarian strategies.

The Rational Appeal of Value Investing

Value investing's appeal is grounded in the idea that markets can misprice assets, creating opportunities for savvy investors to profit from the eventual correction of these mispricings. Value investors seek stocks or assets that are trading below their intrinsic value, often based on financial ratios like price-to-earnings (P/E) or price-to-book (P/B) ratios. This approach seems rational and straightforward, but it is influenced by various psychological factors:

1. Contrarian Thinking: Value investing embraces contrarianism by advocating the purchase of assets that are out of favor with the market. Contrarians often need to swim against the tide of popular sentiment, which can be psychologically challenging.

2. Patience and Delayed Gratification: Value investing requires patience, as it may take time for the market to recognize the true value of an asset. Overcoming the urge for immediate gratification requires psychological discipline.

3. Focus on Fundamentals: Value investors focus on fundamental analysis, relying on objective financial metrics. This emphasis on concrete numbers can counteract emotional decision-making.

The Role of Behavioral Biases

Value investing's success is intrinsically linked to the cognitive biases that influence market behavior. These biases contribute to the mispricing of assets, presenting opportunities for value investors to capitalize on the gap between market price and intrinsic value:

1. **Herding Behavior:** Herd behavior can lead to market overreactions, creating undervalued assets when the market sentiment turns excessively negative.

2. **Loss Aversion:** Investors' aversion to losses can lead to overselling and undervaluation of assets, creating opportunities for value investors to step in.

3. **Availability Bias:** Recent negative news can distort perceptions of an asset's value, causing investors to underestimate its long-term potential.

4. **Anchoring and Adjustment:** Anchoring to a stock's recent high price can create an overly pessimistic view of its potential recovery, leading to undervaluation.

Navigating Value Investing with Psychology

Understanding the psychological dynamics behind value investing can guide investors in effectively applying this strategy:

1. **Emotional Discipline:** Maintaining emotional discipline is crucial in contrarian strategies. Staying focused on fundamentals and long-term goals can help overcome the emotional challenges of going against the crowd.

2. **Information Diversification:** Gather diverse sources of information to form a balanced view of an asset's value. Overreliance on a single piece of negative information can lead to undervaluation.

3. **Patience and Conviction:** Be prepared for a longer investment horizon. The market may not recognize the value immediately, but having conviction in your analysis is essential.

4. Contrarian Bias: Recognize that contrarian strategies carry inherent biases. Avoid falling into the trap of contrarianism for its own sake; ensure your investments are backed by solid fundamentals.

5. Risk Management: While value investing can be lucrative, it's not immune to risks. Diversification and risk management are crucial to mitigate the impact of potential misjudgments.

6. Continuous Learning: Stay informed about behavioral biases and their impact on market trends. This knowledge can inform your decision-making and help you navigate market fluctuations.

7. Flexibility: Be willing to adjust your value investment approach when new information emerges. The ability to adapt to changing circumstances is essential.

A Symphony of Rationality and Psychology

Value investing beautifully illustrates the interplay between rational analysis and psychological influences in the world of finance. As investors delve into the depths of fundamental analysis and uncover hidden value, they must also navigate the psychological biases that create opportunities for mispriced assets. By acknowledging and embracing the psychological factors at play, value investors can capitalize on market inefficiencies, cultivate discipline, and ultimately achieve the coveted goal of buying assets at a discount and selling them at a premium.

Growth Investing: The Psychological Allure of High-Growth Potential

Growth investing, a strategy centered on identifying and investing in companies with significant growth potential, captivates investors with the promise of substantial returns. It's a strategy that embraces innovation, expansion, and the allure of companies that are poised to dominate their markets. However, behind the numbers and projections lies a fascinating interplay of psychology and investor behavior. This chapter delves into the psychological factors that underlie growth investing, exploring the allure of high-growth potential, the cognitive biases that contribute to its appeal, and the challenges of managing expectations in a rapidly evolving landscape.

The Appeal of Growth Investing

At its core, growth investing resonates with the allure of the unknown and the anticipation of future success. Here's why growth investing holds such strong psychological appeal:

1. **Hope and Optimism:** Growth investing is inherently forward-looking, appealing to investors' sense of hope and optimism about a company's potential.

2. **Future Dominance:** The prospect of investing in a company that could become a dominant player in its industry is emotionally enticing.

3. **Innovation and Progress:** Growth companies often embody innovation and progress, tapping into investors' desire to be associated with cutting-edge advancements.

4. **Narrative and Storytelling:** Growth investing is often accompanied by compelling narratives of disruption and transformation, captivating investors' imagination.

The Role of Behavioral Biases

Growth investing thrives on cognitive biases that shape investor behavior and market dynamics. Understanding these biases sheds light on why growth investing can lead to both remarkable successes and challenges:

1. **Confirmation Bias:** Investors seek information that confirms their belief in a company's growth prospects, reinforcing their commitment to the investment.

2. **Optimism Bias:** Investors tend to overestimate the likelihood of positive outcomes, fueling their confidence in the growth potential of the invested company.

3. **Anchoring and Adjustment:** Anchoring to a company's recent achievements can lead to an overestimation of its future growth trajectory.

4. Illusion of Knowledge: The more investors learn about a company's growth prospects, the more confident they may become in their predictions, leading to an illusion of superior knowledge.

Navigating Growth Investing with Psychology

Understanding the psychological drivers of growth investing can help investors navigate the complexities of high-growth potential:

1. Balance Expectations: Temper optimism with a realistic assessment of potential risks and challenges that growth companies may face.

2. Diversification: While growth companies can be exciting, diversification across industries and sectors can help manage risk.

3. Long-Term Perspective: Growth investing requires a long-term horizon. Prepare to weather short-term volatility in pursuit of long-term potential.

4. Fundamental Analysis: Combine the excitement of growth potential with rigorous fundamental analysis to assess a company's true prospects.

5. Information Evaluation: Evaluate information critically. Avoid confirmation bias by seeking out contrary opinions and perspectives.

6. Risk Management: Be aware that not all growth companies succeed. Implement risk management strategies to protect your investment portfolio.

7. Continual Monitoring: Stay vigilant about changes in a growth company's fundamentals and competitive landscape. Adjust your investment thesis as needed.

8. Mind the Hype: Be cautious of excessive hype and speculation. A compelling narrative doesn't always translate into sustainable growth.

A Balancing Act of Dreams and Reality

Growth investing embodies the intersection of aspiration and analytical rigor. Investors are drawn to the potential of riding the wave of innovation and advancement, but success requires a delicate balance between the allure of high-growth potential and the realities of market dynamics. By recognizing the psychological biases that influence growth investing and pairing them with thorough research and a disciplined approach, investors can harness the excitement of the unknown while making informed decisions that align with their investment goals and risk tolerance.

Behavioral Aspects of Technical Analysis: Understanding Price Patterns and Trends

Technical analysis, a widely used approach in financial markets, relies on the examination of historical price patterns and trends to make predictions about future price movements. While technical analysis appears to be rooted in numbers and charts, its effectiveness is deeply influenced by the psychological dynamics of market participants. This chapter delves into the behavioral aspects of technical analysis, exploring how cognitive biases, investor sentiment, and collective behavior contribute to the formation of price patterns and trends, and how understanding these psychological factors can enhance the application of technical analysis strategies.

The Role of Psychology in Technical Analysis

Technical analysis operates on the premise that historical price patterns and trends reflect the collective psychology of market participants. This psychology-driven approach is based on several key principles:

1. Price Reflects All Information: Technical analysts believe that all available information, including psychological factors, is already reflected in the price of an asset.

2. Patterns Reveal Psychology: Patterns, such as head and shoulders or double tops, are believed to represent recurring psychological behavior of market participants.

3. Investor Sentiment Matters: Technical analysis acknowledges that investor sentiment can be a powerful force in driving price movements.

Cognitive Biases and Technical Patterns

Cognitive biases, the inherent mental shortcuts and patterns that affect decision-making, play a substantial role in the formation of technical patterns:

1. **Confirmation Bias:** Traders may seek out technical patterns that confirm their pre-existing beliefs about an asset's direction.

2. **Anchoring and Adjustment:** Traders might anchor to previous price levels and adjust their expectations accordingly.

3. **Herding Behavior:** When a technical pattern forms, herding behavior can lead to exaggerated price movements as traders act in unison.

Patterns and Emotional Responses

Technical patterns and trends can evoke emotional responses among traders, further impacting market dynamics:

1. **Breakouts and Breakdowns:** The excitement of a breakout or the fear of a breakdown can trigger rapid price movements as traders react emotionally.

2. **Resistance and Support Levels:** Psychological levels, such as resistance and support, can influence trader decisions, leading to trend continuation or reversal.

3. **Trend Confirmation:** The confirmation of a trend through technical indicators can fuel emotional trading decisions.

Navigating Technical Analysis with Psychology

Understanding the psychological elements that underpin technical analysis can enhance traders' effectiveness in using this approach:

1. **Emotional Discipline:** Recognize the emotional impact of patterns and trends. Emotional discipline is key to making rational decisions.

2. **Objectivity:** Use technical analysis as a tool for objective analysis, not as a means to confirm emotional biases.

3. Combining Fundamentals and Technicals: Pair technical analysis with fundamental analysis to create a comprehensive view of an asset's potential.

4. Context Matters: Consider the broader market environment and news events that could impact price patterns and trends.

5. Risk Management: Employ sound risk management techniques to avoid being swayed solely by the allure of technical patterns.

6. Continuous Learning: Stay informed about cognitive biases and their impact on technical analysis. This knowledge can enhance your analytical skills.

7. Flexibility: Be willing to adjust your analysis when new information emerges. Psychology-driven trends can shift suddenly.

A Symphony of Psychology and Price Movements

Technical analysis is not a mere exercise in chart patterns; it's a dynamic interplay between the collective psychology of market participants and the resulting price patterns and trends. By acknowledging the role of cognitive biases, investor sentiment, and emotional responses in shaping technical patterns, traders can apply this approach more effectively. Technical analysis becomes a fascinating exploration of human behavior in financial markets, where understanding the psychology behind the numbers can lead to more informed and rational trading decisions.

Chapter 6: Prospect Theory and Investment Decisions

Reference Point Effects: How Investment Decisions are Influenced by Starting Points

Prospect theory, a cornerstone of behavioral finance, introduces the concept of reference points—the starting points from which individuals evaluate potential gains and losses. This chapter explores how reference point effects play a pivotal role in shaping investment decisions, leading to behavior that deviates from traditional economic models. By understanding how reference points influence risk perception, investment choices, and reactions to market volatility, investors can gain insights into their own decision-making processes and make more informed financial choices.

The Essence of Prospect Theory

At the heart of prospect theory is the recognition that individuals do not evaluate potential outcomes in isolation. Instead, they compare outcomes against a reference point, which serves as a baseline for assessing gains and losses. This theory introduced two key concepts:

1. Loss Aversion: People tend to experience losses more intensely than gains of the same magnitude. Loss aversion is a powerful psychological phenomenon that affects investment decisions.

2. Diminishing Sensitivity: As wealth increases, additional gains have diminishing impact on overall well-being. Similarly, additional losses have diminishing impact on distress.

Reference Point Effects in Investment Decisions

The influence of reference points extends into various aspects of investment decision-making:

1. **Risk Perception:** Reference points influence how investors perceive risk. An investment below the reference point is often seen as more risky than an equivalent investment above it.

2. **Herding Behavior:** Investors may follow prevailing trends as they aim to surpass a reference point set by others.

3. **Framing:** How an investment decision is framed—whether in terms of potential gains or potential losses—can significantly impact choices.

4. **Mental Accounting:** Investors compartmentalize their investments into mental accounts, each with its own reference point.

5. **Sunk Cost Fallacy:** People may hold onto investments that have fallen below the reference point due to reluctance to realize losses.

Investment Strategies and Reference Points

Reference point effects play a pivotal role in shaping investment strategies and approaches:

1. **Risk-Taking Behavior:** Investors may become more risk-averse as their investments approach a reference point, avoiding potential losses.

2. **Holding onto Losers:** The reluctance to realize losses can lead to holding onto underperforming investments to avoid admitting mistakes.

3. **Performance Evaluation:** Investors evaluate their portfolio's performance based on how it fares relative to a chosen benchmark—a reference point.

4. **Goal Setting:** Setting financial goals creates reference points that influence savings, spending, and investment decisions.

Mitigating Reference Point Biases

Understanding the influence of reference points on investment decisions can aid investors in making more rational choices:

1. **Awareness:** Be aware of how reference points may be impacting your decision-making. Recognize when you're considering gains and losses relative to a baseline.

2. **Diversification:** Diversify your investments to reduce the impact of any single reference point on your overall portfolio.

3. **Long-Term Perspective:** Set long-term goals to create reference points that align with your overall financial objectives.

4. **Reevaluate Goals:** Regularly reevaluate your financial goals and reference points to ensure they remain relevant and realistic.

5. **Avoid Sunk Cost Fallacy:** Make investment decisions based on current and future prospects, rather than past decisions.

6. **Seek Professional Advice:** Financial advisors can provide an objective perspective, helping you make decisions that align with your goals.

The Influence of Starting Points

Reference point effects highlight the intricacies of human decision-making in financial contexts. By acknowledging that investment decisions are influenced by where we start—our reference points—investors can gain a deeper understanding of why they make certain choices. This awareness empowers individuals to make more deliberate, rational, and well-informed investment decisions that align with their goals and aspirations.

Endowment Effect: The Bias towards Valuing Assets We Own More than Those We Don't

The endowment effect, a prominent cognitive bias in behavioral finance, reveals a fascinating aspect of human psychology in relation to ownership and valuation. This chapter delves into the intricacies of the endowment effect and how it influences financial decisions, investment choices, and market dynamics. By understanding this bias, investors can gain insights into the emotional and psychological factors that shape their perception of value, leading to more informed and rational decision-making.

Understanding the Endowment Effect

The endowment effect highlights the psychological phenomenon where individuals tend to value items they own more than equivalent items they do not own. This tendency runs counter to traditional economic theories, which assume that people should value items based on their objective attributes rather than their ownership status.

Ownership and Valuation

The endowment effect stems from a combination of factors related to ownership and the psychological attachment to possessions:

1. **Loss Aversion:** Individuals feel a sense of loss when parting with items they own, leading to an inflated perception of their value.

2. **Psychological Ownership:** The act of owning something creates a psychological attachment that influences how it's valued.

3. **Status Quo Bias:** People tend to prefer maintaining their current ownership status, which can lead to overvaluing owned assets.

4. **Cognitive Dissonance:** Valuing owned items more highly helps reconcile the discomfort of potential loss with the desire for consistency.

Implications for Financial Decisions

The endowment effect has significant implications for various financial decisions and market dynamics:

1. **Investment Choices:** Investors may overvalue assets in their portfolio, making them reluctant to sell even if more financially sound options exist.

2. **Pricing Discrepancies:** The endowment effect contributes to pricing discrepancies in financial markets, where buyers and sellers perceive different values.

3. Market Bubbles: The collective influence of the endowment effect can contribute to the formation of market bubbles as prices exceed rational valuations.

4. Mergers and Acquisitions: The endowment effect can lead to overvaluing one's own company and undervaluing potential acquisition targets.

5. Consumer Behavior: The bias affects purchasing decisions, where consumers may attach higher value to products they own.

Mitigating the Endowment Effect

Understanding the endowment effect is the first step toward mitigating its impact on financial decisions:

1. Objectivity: Approach decisions with objectivity, recognizing that ownership should not inherently influence valuation.

2. External Perspective: Imagine valuing the asset from an outsider's point of view to counteract the bias.

3. Diversification: Diversify your investments to reduce the emotional attachment to any single asset.

4. Regular Reevaluation: Regularly reassess your portfolio with a critical eye to avoid clinging to overvalued assets.

5. Emotional Awareness: Be aware of the emotional connection you have to owned assets and its potential impact on decision-making.

6. Seek Expert Advice: Financial advisors can provide an unbiased perspective, helping you objectively evaluate the value of your assets.

Value through an Objective Lens

The endowment effect highlights the profound influence of psychological attachment on our financial decisions. By recognizing this bias, investors can strive for more objective and rational valuations, allowing them to make decisions that align with their financial goals rather than emotional attachments.

Embracing objectivity over ownership-driven valuation empowers individuals to navigate financial landscapes with a clearer understanding of value and an increased ability to make well-informed choices.

Chapter 7: Herd Behavior and Crowd Dynamics

Framing Effects: How the Presentation of Information Affects Decision-Making

Framing effects, a pivotal concept in behavioral finance, shed light on how the way information is presented can significantly impact decision-making. This chapter delves into the complexities of framing effects and their profound influence on financial choices, market trends, and investor behavior. By understanding how the framing of information can lead to different perceptions and decisions, individuals can become more aware of their own biases and make more objective and informed financial choices.

The Power of Framing

Framing effects underscore the idea that the same information, when presented in different ways, can evoke contrasting responses due to the way it is framed. This phenomenon is central to behavioral finance, as it highlights the subjectivity inherent in decision-making processes.

Positive vs. Negative Framing

Framing effects often manifest through positive and negative framing:

1. **Positive Framing:** Information is presented in terms of potential gains, focusing on the benefits and positive outcomes.

2. **Negative Framing:** Information is presented in terms of potential losses, highlighting the drawbacks and negative consequences.

Examples of Framing Effects

Framing effects are pervasive in various financial contexts:

1. **Investment Choices:** How an investment is framed can influence perceived risk and return, affecting the decision to invest or not.

2. Risk Perception: Information presented in terms of losses may heighten risk aversion, while gains-focused framing can encourage risk-taking.

3. Savings Decisions: Framing can impact decisions related to saving for retirement or other long-term goals.

4. Consumer Behavior: Framing can influence consumer decisions, affecting choices from product purchases to investment options.

5. Market Sentiment: The media's framing of market news can influence investor sentiment and impact market trends.

Mitigating Framing Effects

Awareness and critical thinking are key in mitigating the impact of framing effects on decision-making:

1. Objectivity: Recognize the potential influence of framing on your decisions and strive for objective evaluation.

2. Information Seeking: Gather information from multiple sources to gain a comprehensive view of the situation.

3. Consider Both Sides: Consider how information might be framed differently and analyze the implications of each framing.

4. Question Assumptions: Question the assumptions underlying the framing of information to uncover potential biases.

5. Emotional Awareness: Be aware of emotional responses that certain framings may trigger and evaluate decisions rationally.

6. Consult Professionals: Seek advice from financial professionals who can provide an objective perspective on the framing of information.

The Subjectivity of Perception

Framing effects exemplify the subjective nature of human perception and decision-making. By understanding how the presentation of information can shape our choices, investors can take steps to ensure that their decisions are driven by rational evaluation rather than the influence of framing biases. Striving for objectivity and critical thinking when evaluating information helps individuals navigate the intricate landscape of finance with greater clarity and autonomy.

Bandwagon Effect: The Impact of Consensus on Individual Investment Choices

In the realm of behavioral finance, the bandwagon effect stands as a testament to the power of consensus and its impact on shaping individual investment decisions. Chapter 7 uncovers the intricate dynamics of the bandwagon effect, revealing how the collective behavior of investors can drive market trends and influence individual choices. By examining the psychological mechanisms at play, this chapter equips readers with insights to navigate the alluring but potentially risky world of following the crowd.

Riding the Bandwagon

The bandwagon effect illustrates how individuals tend to conform to prevailing trends, believing that joining the majority is a safe and wise decision. It stems from the desire for social validation, the fear of missing out, and the assumption that the majority's choices are better informed.

The Dynamics of Consensus

The bandwagon effect leads to several dynamics in the investment landscape:

1. Positive Feedback Loop: As more investors jump on a trend, the trend gains momentum, creating a self-reinforcing cycle.

2. Influence on Prices: Increased demand due to the bandwagon effect can lead to price hikes, often detached from underlying fundamentals.

3. Crowded Trades: The influx of investors into a specific asset class or investment strategy can create overcrowding and subsequent risks.

Psychological Drivers

The bandwagon effect is rooted in cognitive biases and emotional responses:

1. Social Proof: The idea that others' decisions validate our own choices, leading to conformity.

2. Fear of Regret: The fear of missing out or making a different choice than the majority can drive herd behavior.

3. Reduced Cognitive Effort: Following the crowd requires less cognitive effort than independent analysis.

Navigating the Bandwagon Effect

Awareness and strategic thinking are vital to counteracting the bandwagon effect:

1. Independent Analysis: Base investment decisions on thorough research and analysis, rather than succumbing to herd behavior.

2. Contrarian Approach: Occasionally taking a contrarian stance can present opportunities when consensus is misplaced.

3. Long-Term Perspective: Prioritize long-term goals and fundamentals over short-term trends driven by the bandwagon effect.

4. Emotional Regulation: Embrace emotional intelligence to prevent rash decisions influenced by crowd dynamics.

5. Diversification: Diversifying across asset classes can mitigate risks associated with overexposure to a particular trend.

6. Information Verification: Validate information from reliable sources before making investment decisions based on the consensus.

A Balanced Approach

The bandwagon effect underscores the fascinating interplay between psychology and financial markets. By grasping the psychology behind this phenomenon, investors can navigate investment landscapes with prudence and discernment. Striving for balance between following the crowd and making informed, independent choices ensures that individuals capitalize on opportunities while preserving their financial well-being. The bandwagon may be tempting, but with awareness, investors can transcend its influence and embark on a more enlightened investment journey.

Anti-Herding Behavior: Recognizing When Contrarian Strategies Deviate from the Crowd

In a landscape often dominated by herd behavior and consensus-driven choices, understanding how to recognize and strategically deviate from the crowd is a skill that can lead to unique opportunities and improved risk management. By exploring the psychology and mechanics of anti-herding, readers gain insights into how to make investment decisions that stand apart from the mainstream.

The Essence of Anti-Herding

Anti-herding stands in stark contrast to herd behavior, emphasizing the importance of independent analysis and the willingness to deviate from the crowd. It involves making decisions that go against prevailing market trends, driven by the conviction that consensus is not always accurate or rational.

Recognizing Contrarian Signals

Effectively practicing anti-herding involves recognizing signals that indicate deviation from the crowd may be warranted:

1. Overcrowding: Overcrowded trades or asset classes can indicate the need for a contrarian stance.

2. Excessive Optimism or Pessimism: Extreme market sentiment often signals a potential reversal, making a contrarian approach valuable.

3. Valuation Disparities: Contrarian opportunities can arise when an asset is undervalued or overvalued relative to its fundamentals.

Psychological Foundations

The psychology behind anti-herding is based on a few key principles:

1. Independent Thinking: Anti-herders prioritize independent analysis over the desire to conform.

2. Emotional Resilience: They remain emotionally resilient when their decisions deviate from the majority.

3. Risk Management: Anti-herding can be driven by a desire to manage risk by avoiding overcrowded trades.

Benefits and Challenges

Anti-herding comes with its own set of benefits and challenges:

Benefits:

1. Unique Opportunities: Contrarian strategies can uncover undervalued assets and opportunities overlooked by the crowd.

2. Improved Risk Management: Anti-herding helps mitigate risks associated with crowded trades and overexposure.

3. Long-Term Perspective: Contrarian investors often have a long-term focus, prioritizing fundamentals over short-term trends.

Challenges:

1. Uncertainty: Deviating from the crowd can feel uncertain and lead to occasional periods of underperformance.

2. Timing: Timing contrarian moves can be challenging, as it involves predicting when sentiment will shift.

3. Emotional Resilience: Being contrarian requires emotional resilience to withstand potential criticism or skepticism.

Navigating Anti-Herding

Successfully navigating anti-herding requires a balanced approach:

1. **Research and Analysis:** Conduct thorough research to ensure your contrarian stance is based on solid fundamentals.

2. **Patience:** Contrarian moves may take time to materialize, requiring patience and a long-term perspective.

3. **Risk Management:** Use anti-herding as part of a comprehensive risk management strategy.

4. **Emotional Discipline:** Develop emotional discipline to remain committed to your contrarian convictions.

5. **Continuous Learning:** Stay informed about market dynamics and trends that could signal contrarian opportunities.

Harnessing Individuality

Anti-herding exemplifies the power of individuality in the world of finance. By recognizing when to deviate from consensus and embrace a contrarian approach, investors can unlock unique opportunities and reduce risks associated with herd behavior. Balancing the desire to stand apart from the crowd with diligent research and strategic decision-making empowers investors to harness the power of anti-herding and navigate financial markets with insight and confidence.

Chapter 8: Emotional Biases and Risk Management

Loss Aversion and Risk Tolerance: Navigating the Challenge of Emotions and Risk Exposure

By exploring the psychological mechanisms behind loss aversion and risk tolerance, this chapter provides readers with insights into how to navigate the emotional complexities of investing while maintaining a balanced and rational approach to risk management.

The Emotional Quandary

Loss aversion and risk tolerance often lead to an emotional tug-of-war for investors, as they grapple with their inherent aversion to losses and their desire for gains. Balancing these conflicting emotions is a critical aspect of successful risk management.

Understanding Loss Aversion

Loss aversion refers to the psychological tendency to feel the pain of losses more acutely than the pleasure of gains. This bias can lead investors to make irrational decisions driven by the desire to avoid losses rather than to achieve gains.

Impact on Risk Tolerance

Loss aversion can significantly impact an individual's risk tolerance:

1. **Risk Aversion:** Loss aversion can lead to a lower willingness to take on risks, as investors are more focused on avoiding losses than pursuing gains.

2. **Short-Term Focus:** Investors driven by loss aversion may prioritize short-term stability over long-term growth.

3. **Anxiety and Stress:** Loss aversion can lead to increased anxiety and stress when facing volatile market conditions.

Balancing Risk and Emotions

Effectively managing loss aversion and risk tolerance involves striking a delicate balance:

1. **Risk Education:** Educating oneself about different types of risks can help individuals make more informed decisions.

2. **Long-Term Perspective:** Focusing on long-term goals can help mitigate the impact of short-term losses.

3. **Diversification:** Diversifying a portfolio can help reduce the impact of losses from any single investment.

4. **Financial Planning:** Developing a comprehensive financial plan can provide a structured approach to risk management.

Overcoming Loss Aversion

Overcoming loss aversion requires a blend of emotional intelligence and rational decision-making:

1. **Emotion Regulation:** Developing emotional resilience and learning to manage the emotional impact of losses is crucial.

2. **Behavioral Coaching:** Professional guidance can help investors navigate emotional challenges and make rational decisions.

3. **Simulation Exercises:** Practicing simulated investment scenarios can help individuals experience loss in a controlled environment, reducing its emotional impact.

4. **Goal Alignment:** Aligning investment decisions with personal financial goals can help put losses in perspective.

Risk Tolerance Assessment

Understanding one's risk tolerance and its alignment with loss aversion is fundamental:

1. **Risk Profiling:** Assessing one's risk tolerance using psychological tools can provide valuable insights.

2. Realistic Expectations: Setting realistic expectations about potential losses and gains can mitigate the impact of loss aversion.

3. Regular Review: Continuously reviewing and adjusting risk tolerance as financial circumstances evolve is essential.

Emotionally Intelligent Risk Management

By acknowledging the impact of loss aversion on risk tolerance and adopting strategies to manage these emotions, investors can strike a harmonious balance between their emotional responses and their rational decisions. The journey towards mastering emotional biases and risk tolerance is a key component of becoming a more resilient and strategic investor in the ever-changing landscape of financial markets.

Mental Accounting: Segmenting Investments and Its Influence on Risk Perception

By exploring how individuals mentally categorize their investments, this chapter unveils the complexities of risk assessment and decision-making that arise from these cognitive divisions. Readers gain valuable insights into how mental accounting shapes our financial choices and how understanding this phenomenon can lead to more informed and balanced risk management strategies.

The Concept of Mental Accounting

Mental accounting refers to the cognitive habit of segregating financial resources into distinct mental compartments. Instead of viewing wealth as a single pool, individuals partition their investments into separate accounts based on factors such as purpose, source, or even emotional significance.

Impact on Risk Perception

Mental accounting has a significant influence on how individuals perceive and respond to risk:

1. **Risk Segmentation:** Investments assigned to different mental accounts are perceived with varying degrees of risk, even if they belong to the same portfolio.

2. **Loss Aversion Variation:** Losses in certain mental accounts may trigger more intense emotions due to their designated purpose or significance.

3. **Altered Risk-Return Tradeoff:** Different mental accounts can lead to a distortion of the risk-return tradeoff, affecting investment decisions.

Segmentation Mechanisms

Mental accounting manifests through several mechanisms:

1. **Budgeting:** Allocating funds for specific purposes, such as retirement, education, or leisure.

2. **Source Differentiation:** Treating money from different sources (e.g., salary, bonus) differently.

3. **Time Frame:** Separating investments based on short-term or long-term objectives.

Pros and Cons

Mental accounting offers both benefits and drawbacks:

Benefits:

1. **Financial Discipline:** Segmentation can encourage disciplined savings and spending behavior.

2. **Goal-Oriented Focus:** Mental accounts align with specific financial goals, fostering purposeful financial decisions.

3. **Emotional Satisfaction:** Achieving milestones within specific mental accounts can provide emotional satisfaction.

Drawbacks:

1. Suboptimal Allocation: Segmentation can lead to suboptimal allocation if it ignores overall portfolio diversification.

2. Emotional Biases: Mental accounts can amplify emotional biases, influencing decisions without considering the broader picture.

3. Limited Flexibility: Fixed mental accounts may not adapt well to changing financial circumstances.

Strategies for Effective Mental Accounting

To harness the benefits of mental accounting while mitigating its drawbacks, investors can adopt thoughtful strategies:

1. Holistic Perspective: Continuously remind oneself of the comprehensive portfolio context, not just individual mental accounts.

2. Periodic Review: Regularly reassess and adjust mental accounts to align with evolving financial goals.

3. Diversification: Focus on portfolio diversification rather than overemphasizing the performance of individual mental accounts.

4. Emotional Awareness: Recognize the influence of mental accounts on emotional biases and decision-making.

5. Flexible Adaptation: Be open to modifying mental accounts to accommodate changes in financial circumstances.

Embracing Balanced Risk Perception

By understanding how mental compartments can lead to distorted risk assessment and decision-making, investors gain the tools to navigate their financial landscape with greater insight. By employing strategies that align mental accounting with a comprehensive portfolio perspective, readers can embrace a more balanced and informed approach to risk management, ultimately leading to more effective financial outcomes.

Ambiguity Aversion: Navigating Uncertainty in Decisions and Risk Management

By exploring the complexities of ambiguity and its effects on investor behavior, this chapter offers readers a profound understanding of how individuals navigate the unknown and make choices in the face of limited information. Through this exploration, readers gain insights into the psychological mechanisms that drive ambiguity aversion and strategies to effectively manage its impact.

Decoding Ambiguity Aversion

Ambiguity aversion refers to the psychological inclination to avoid situations where the level of uncertainty is high and the probabilities are unclear. This bias stems from the human desire to seek clarity and reduce cognitive dissonance in decision-making.

The Impact on Investment Decisions

Ambiguity aversion significantly influences investment decisions:

1. **Conservative Choices:** Ambiguity-averse individuals tend to opt for safer, known options over those with uncertain outcomes.

2. **Risk Avoidance:** Ambiguity aversion can lead to a higher aversion to risk, even if the potential returns are attractive.

3. **Influence on Portfolios:** Portfolios of ambiguity-averse investors may lean towards assets with more predictable outcomes.

Understanding the Ellsberg Paradox

The Ellsberg paradox, a classic experiment, highlights ambiguity aversion:

1. **Known vs. Unknown:** Participants often prefer betting on known probabilities rather than uncertain ones.

2. **Preference for Certainty:** Individuals display a preference for information that provides certainty, even when it doesn't improve the odds of success.

3. Impact on Choices: The paradox underscores how ambiguity aversion influences choices and risk perception.

The Role of Framing

Framing, or the way information is presented, plays a pivotal role in ambiguity aversion:

1. Positive vs. Negative Framing: Ambiguity aversion can lead to a preference for positively framed choices to avoid uncertain losses.

2. Information Processing: Ambiguity-averse individuals may process negative information differently to minimize the cognitive discomfort of uncertainty.

Strategies to Navigate Ambiguity Aversion

Effectively managing ambiguity aversion requires strategic approaches:

1. Information Seeking: Gathering more information can help reduce ambiguity and provide a more informed basis for decision-making.

2. Rational Evaluation: Encourage rational evaluation of potential outcomes and probabilities, even in the face of uncertainty.

3. Diversification: Diversifying investments can mitigate the impact of ambiguous outcomes on the overall portfolio.

4. Long-Term Focus: Focusing on long-term investment goals can alleviate the short-term discomfort caused by ambiguity.

5. Emotional Awareness: Recognizing the emotional discomfort associated with ambiguity can help individuals make more balanced decisions.

Navigating Uncertainty in Risk Management

By understanding the cognitive biases that drive ambiguity aversion, readers are equipped to approach ambiguous situations with greater awareness and strategic insight. Armed with strategies to address ambiguity's impact, investors can make more confident, rational choices that align with their financial goals and objectives.

Chapter 9: Behavioral Portfolio Management

Building a Behaviorally-Aware Portfolio: Integrating Psychological Insights

This chapter explores how understanding investor behavior and cognitive biases can shape the construction and management of portfolios. By uncovering the ways in which behavioral factors influence decision-making and asset allocation, readers gain valuable tools to build portfolios that align with individual financial goals while accounting for the quirks of human psychology.

Behavioral Portfolio Management: The Intersection of Psychology and Finance

Behavioral portfolio management is the art of constructing portfolios that are designed with a deep understanding of how psychological biases impact investment decisions. This chapter introduces readers to the concept and highlights its significance in the modern financial landscape.

Applying Behavioral Insights

The chapter dives into the practical application of behavioral insights in portfolio management:

1. **Biased Decision-Making:** Understand how cognitive biases influence investment choices and result in suboptimal decision-making.

2. **Emotional Impacts:** Recognize the emotional aspects of investing and how they can drive impulsive decisions or hinder rational choices.

3. **Investor Types:** Explore different investor personality types and tailor portfolios to suit their behavioral tendencies.

Building a Behaviorally-Aware Portfolio

The heart of the chapter centers around the process of constructing portfolios that incorporate psychological insights:

1. Asset Allocation: Learn how to adjust asset allocations based on investor risk profiles and behavioral biases.

2. Goal Setting: Align portfolio goals with investor aspirations, reducing the potential for emotional decisions during market volatility.

3. Behavioral Risk Management: Develop strategies that counteract the impact of cognitive biases on risk perception.

4. Communication Strategies: Craft clear and transparent communication to manage client expectations and minimize emotional reactions.

Behavioral Portfolio Strategies

Explore strategies that leverage behavioral insights for portfolio management:

1. Nudging Strategies: Design portfolios that gently nudge investors towards disciplined behavior and long-term focus.

2. Anchoring Mitigation: Counteract the anchoring bias by regularly reassessing portfolio allocations based on evolving market conditions.

3. Mental Accounting Alignment: Harmonize mental accounting divisions with overall portfolio objectives for consistent decision-making.

The Future of Behavioral Portfolio Management

Consider the evolving landscape of behavioral portfolio management:

1. Technological Advancements: Explore how technology can aid in behavioral analysis and portfolio optimization.

2. Ethical Considerations: Delve into the ethical implications of leveraging behavioral insights to manage investor decisions.

3. Research and Innovation: Anticipate ongoing research advancements that deepen our understanding of behavioral finance.

4. Human-Machine Collaboration: Examine the potential synergy between human expertise and machine learning in behavioral portfolio management.

Navigating the Intersection

By merging psychological insights with portfolio construction strategies, investors can craft portfolios that are both technically sound and aligned with individual investor behavior. Armed with a deep understanding of behavioral portfolio management, readers are empowered to construct investment strategies that not only navigate the complexities of the financial markets but also address the nuanced behavioral tendencies of investors.

Tactical Asset Allocation: Adapting Portfolios Based on Market Sentiment

By examining how investor emotions and sentiment impact the allocation of assets within portfolios, this chapter provides a comprehensive understanding of the strategies that can be employed to capitalize on market trends and navigate changing conditions.

Tactical Asset Allocation: A Behavioral Perspective

Tactical asset allocation involves adjusting portfolio allocations based on short-term market conditions and investor sentiment.

Behavioral Drivers of Tactical Asset Allocation

The chapter unravels the psychological factors that drive tactical asset allocation decisions:

1. **Sentiment Swings:** Understand how shifts in market sentiment can lead to rapid changes in portfolio allocation.

2. **Fear and Greed:** Explore the impact of emotions such as fear and greed on investor behavior and tactical allocation.

3. **Herding Behavior:** Recognize the tendency of investors to follow the crowd and the implications for portfolio adjustments.

Strategies for Tactical Asset Allocation

Discover the strategic approaches to tactically adjusting asset allocations:

1. Contrarian Approach: Learn how to exploit market sentiment extremes by adopting a contrarian stance.

2. Momentum Strategy: Explore how momentum-driven strategies capitalize on market trends and sentiment-driven momentum.

3. Volatility-Based Allocation: Understand how portfolio allocation can be guided by market volatility and its implications for sentiment.

4. Adaptive Portfolio Balancing: Develop techniques to automatically rebalance portfolios based on changing market sentiment.

Behavioral Considerations in Tactical Allocation

The chapter delves into the behavioral aspects of tactical asset allocation:

1. Emotional Discipline: Implement strategies that help investors avoid emotional responses to short-term market fluctuations.

2. Avoiding Herd Behavior: Counteract the influence of herding behavior on tactical decisions.

3. Decision Rules: Establish clear decision rules to guide tactical allocation, reducing impulsive decision-making.

4. Communication Strategies: Communicate the rationale behind tactical changes to manage investor expectations.

Challenges and Opportunities

Reflect on the challenges and potential rewards of tactical asset allocation:

1. Overtrading Risk: Recognize the potential for overtrading driven by emotional reactions to market sentiment.

2. Market Timing Considerations: Understand the nuances of timing tactical shifts and the behavioral challenges it presents.

3. Alignment with Long-Term Goals: Ensure that tactical allocation decisions remain aligned with long-term investment objectives.

Navigating the Dynamic Landscape

By understanding the influence of market sentiment and investor behavior on portfolio adjustments, readers gain insights that can enhance their ability to make informed and strategically sound decisions. Armed with the knowledge of behavioral considerations, investors are better prepared to capitalize on opportunities presented by market sentiment swings while staying aligned with their broader financial goals.

Emotional discipline: Strategies to mitigate impulsive decision-making in portfolios.

Emotional discipline is a crucial aspect of successful investing, particularly when considering the behavioral factors that can lead to impulsive decisions. This bullet point highlights the importance of maintaining emotional discipline in the face of market fluctuations and emotional triggers that may tempt investors to deviate from their long-term investment strategies.

Investors often experience moments of heightened emotions, such as fear, greed, and excitement, which can lead to irrational decisions. These emotions can drive investors to buy or sell assets based on short-term market trends, rather than adhering to their carefully crafted investment plans. Emotional discipline involves recognizing these impulses and employing strategies to prevent emotional biases from derailing investment decisions.

One effective approach to emotional discipline is setting clear investment goals and maintaining a long-term perspective. By anchoring decisions to well-defined objectives, investors can better resist the urge to react impulsively to short-term market movements. Additionally, having a well-diversified portfolio that aligns with an individual's risk tolerance and investment horizon can provide a buffer against emotional knee-jerk reactions.

Investors can also benefit from implementing systematic investment processes that reduce the influence of emotions. Automation tools, like dollar-cost averaging or rebalancing, help maintain a consistent investment strategy without succumbing to emotional highs and lows. Regularly reviewing and adjusting the portfolio based on changes in personal circumstances or financial goals can also provide a structured framework for decision-making that minimizes emotional biases.

Furthermore, seeking advice from financial professionals or engaging in peer discussions can provide an external perspective that counters emotional biases. Having a trusted advisor who can offer objective insights can help investors make rational decisions even during periods of market turbulence.

In conclusion, emotional discipline is a key element in effectively managing portfolios and making informed investment decisions. By understanding and acknowledging emotional biases, investors can implement strategies to counteract impulsive behavior, adhere to their long-term objectives, and navigate market fluctuations with a level-headed approach. This approach ensures that investment decisions are driven by sound financial principles rather than short-term emotions, ultimately leading to more consistent and successful investment outcomes.

Chapter 10: Nudging Investor Behavior

In the realm of finance, the decisions we make often shape our financial destinies. But what if there were ways to enhance our decision-making, to navigate the complex world of investments with greater precision and insight? Chapter 10 delves into the fascinating realm of "Nudging Investor Behavior," where the art and science of behavioral economics merge to revolutionize how we approach financial choices.

Behavioral Nudges: Designing Interventions for Smarter Decisions

In the pursuit of smarter investment decisions, behavioral nudges emerge as a beacon of hope. These subtle interventions are designed to gently steer our cognitive biases and tendencies in the right direction. Through real-world examples and research-backed insights, we explore the power of behavioral nudges in shaping our financial behaviors. From overcoming the allure of short-term gains to taming our risk aversion, this section uncovers how small adjustments can yield monumental improvements in our investment outcomes.

Framing Investment Advice: The Art of Communication

Words possess the extraordinary power to mold perceptions and influence choices. This section uncovers the profound impact of communication on investor choices. By dissecting various communication strategies, we reveal how the mere framing of investment advice can alter our decisions. From understanding the psychological underpinnings of how advice is presented to decoding the implications of different tones, this chapter empowers readers to discern the hidden nuances within financial conversations.

Goal-Based Investing: Aligning Strategies with Personal Financial Goals

In the labyrinth of financial markets, the North Star guiding our decisions should always be our personal financial goals. "Goal-Based Investing" elucidates the transformative concept of aligning investment strategies with individual aspirations. Delving into case studies and expert analyses, we navigate the terrain of setting clear financial objectives and crafting investment blueprints that resonate with these goals. Whether it's funding education, achieving retirement dreams, or realizing a legacy, this section illuminates the path towards purpose-driven financial decisions.

Don't miss out!

Visit the website below and you can sign up to receive emails whenever Alex Thompson publishes a new book. There's no charge and no obligation.

https://books2read.com/r/B-A-FEPY-WZANC

BOOKS 2 READ

Connecting independent readers to independent writers.

Also by Alex Thompson

Alex on Finance

Financial Freedom Roadmap - Achieving Early Retirement through the FIRE Movement

The Art of Strategic Innovation

Beyond Cash - The Evolution of Digital Payment Systems and the Future of Money

Preserving Wealth in Inflationary Times - Strategies for Protecting Your Financial Future

Standalone

Side Hustle Success: Unlocking Your Entrepreneurial Potential

Side Hustle Success: The Ultimate Guide to Passive and Financial Freedom

Mastering the Markets: Advanced Trading Strategies for Success and Ethical Trading Practices

Financial Fortitude

Mastering the Art of Upselling

The Financial Bullet Blueprint

Investing Demystified: A Beginner's Guide to Building Wealth in the Stock Market

Real Estate Riches: Building Wealth through Property Investment

How To Succeed as a Freelancer

Navigating Complex Waters: Advanced Strategies in Portfolio Management

Ethics in Quantitative Finance and Algorithmic Trading: Navigating Transparency, Fairness, and Accountability

Behavioral Finance and Investor Psychology

www.ingramcontent.com/pod-product-compliance
Lightning Source LLC
LaVergne TN
LVHW022311200926
848481LV00004B/1292